WHAT ARE THEY FEELING?

Published in 2024 by The School of Life
930 High Road, London, N12 9RT

Copyright © The School of Life 2024
Illustrations © Daniel Gray-Barnett
Designed and typeset by Studio Katie Kerr

Printed in China by Leo Paper Group

The School of Life publishes a range of books on essential
topics in psychological and emotional life, including
relationships, parenting, friendship, careers and fulfilment.
The aim is always to help us to understand ourselves better
– and thereby to grow calmer, less confused and more
purposeful. Discover our full range of titles, including
books for children, here:
www.theschooloflife.com/books

The School of Life also offers a comprehensive
therapy service, which complements, and draws
upon, our published works:
www.theschooloflife.com/therapy

www.theschooloflife.com

Hardback ISBN: 978-1-915087-28-7
Paperback ISBN: 978-1-916753-16-7

10 9 8 7 6 5 4 3 2 1

WHAT ARE THEY FEELING?

The School of Life

Contents

What is this book all about?

This is a book all about lots of different feelings: being sad or excited, upset, pleased, confused, worried, impatient, happy, shy, enthusiastic, frightened, nervous, embarrassed, proud, irritated, calm, jealous, curious, overwhelmed, angry, cheerful or ... well, there are so many different feelings, we couldn't possibly list them all!

But mostly this book isn't about *your* feelings; it's about the feelings of *other people*. And that makes a big difference. It's important to think about what others might be feeling, so we can understand the people around us better and be a good friend.

Most of the time you automatically know what your feelings are, *from the inside*. But when it comes to other people, they might not always tell you how they really feel: you need to work out what they might be feeling, *from the outside*. And that's not so easy.

Finding out what someone is feeling is like being a detective. You need to look for clues. And you need to keep an open mind. You can't be *sure* how another person feels, but being interested in trying to work it out shows that you care.

Detective Feelings

Introducing Detective Feelings! Detective Feelings looks for clues about how someone is feeling. Take a look at this picture. What do you think the child in the turquoise T-shirt might be feeling? What would Detective Feelings do in this situation?

First, Detective Feelings might look at the person: Are they smiling? Are they frowning? Do they look like they want to cry? Are they jumping up and down or standing very still?

Next, they might think about what's been happening around them, to help them understand the person's situation: Has someone else been telling a joke or saying something a bit mean? Has a grown-up just said 'no' or told them off? Are they about to try something new? Or are they holding something that might give a clue to what's happening?

The clues seem pretty clear in this case: the child's toy has broken, and they are sad. But understanding someone's feelings is not always so obvious.

9

Now let's turn our detective skills to another case. What might the girl in green be feeling? It *looks* like she's happy: she's got a big smile. Perhaps someone told a joke, said something lovely or she is just really happy in that moment.

Detective Feelings is pretty clever. They know that *sometimes* people smile even when they aren't really happy at all. Have you ever done a fake smile to cover up your real feelings?

Maybe she's smiling because someone has just told a really awful joke, but she is pretending she found it funny to be kind. Or *maybe* she is smiling to hide the fact that she has no idea what another person is talking about. Have you ever just nodded and smiled when a grown-up is talking about something you don't understand or something a bit boring?

Maybe Detective Feelings needs to investigate further ...

Detective Feelings also looks at a person's body language for clues to how they are feeling.

Body language is a way that people communicate with each other without using words. A person's movements, posture (the way someone stands or sits), facial expressions and eyes might reveal more about how they feel. You can see whether their body language matches their smile.

People can smile for so many different reasons. (If you wrote down all the reasons you might smile, it could be a long list and maybe writing it would make you smile quite a few times!)

Here's a classic case for Detective Feelings. This is one of the most famous paintings in the world. It's called the *Mona Lisa*.

The *Mona Lisa* was painted more than 500 years ago by the artist Leonardo da Vinci. It's a very well-known picture, but it's also very mysterious. People have had many different ideas about what the woman is feeling, and even grown-up experts can't agree. This just goes to show how hard it can be to be sure of what someone else is feeling.

What do you think she might be feeling? Have a look and see how many different ideas you can come up with. Look at her eyes and her mouth. You don't need to be sure – you're just suggesting possibilities.

She might be feeling:

- **proud** because she's being painted by da Vinci.
- **relaxed** because she's sitting down on a chair.
- **bored** but is trying not to show it.
- **annoyed** because da Vinci is taking such a long time!
- **embarrassed** that people will stare at her picture.
- **anxious** because she's holding in a sneeze and doesn't want to disturb da Vinci's concentration.

There are so many possibilities – and she might be feeling more than one thing. Have you ever found it annoying when people *think* they know what you must be feeling? Maybe they think you must be enjoying school, or you must hate doing your homework, or that you must love sport, or you must be looking forward to a holiday. Wouldn't it be nicer if they just *wondered* what you might be feeling instead? Or even asked you?

Detective Feelings is great: they are interested in what other people are feeling, but they *know they don't have all the answers*. They're interested in all the possible things someone might be feeling. Their favourite word, as you have maybe guessed, is *might*.

It's very important to not jump to conclusions about other people's feelings. In the case of Mona Lisa, we will never know how she was feeling when she was being painted (unless you were to invent a time machine and go and ask her!). In real life, it's best to gather all the clues about what someone might be feeling. To find out more we could ask the person some questions.

A special word: Empathy

Let's talk about a special word: *empathy*. It means imagining what someone else is feeling – even though you might not feel the same way.

Suppose your friend breaks their arm. Your arm is fine, but you can imagine how much their arm is hurting them and how annoying it would be not to be able to use it – so you ask if they need help with anything and are very careful not to bump into them. Ouch!

Or maybe you're going on a really exciting holiday, but your best friend is staying at home. You can imagine what it feels like for them: maybe they'll be bored, maybe they'll feel they're missing out. You're happy about your trip away, but you realise they might be sad. So, you buy a gift on holiday to tell them that you were thinking about them.

With empathy, you don't have the actual feeling another person has, but with your detective skills, you try very hard to imagine what it is. It's a very kind thing to do. You can care about *their* feelings even though they're not the same as *your* feelings.

Imagine you're playing with your friends and you see another child standing alone. Can you *empathise* with them? What would Detective Feelings do in this situation? They might imagine how they would feel in that position.

What do you think the child might be feeling? If you were standing on your own and you could see other children playing together maybe you would feel lonely, or like you wish you could join in but feel too shy to ask. Perhaps that is how the child is feeling. You can empathise with them using your imagination or your own experiences. Maybe you know how it feels to be shy sometimes.

But it's important to remember that you don't *know* that's how they are really feeling. It's just a guess. Someone else may feel very differently to you in the same situation. You can only base your response on your best guess at how the other person is feeling.

What *is* sympathy?

There's another word for understanding what someone else is feeling: it's *sympathy*. Sympathy is when you are able to understand another person's feelings because you feel the same way. If you join a new club and are a bit shy about not knowing anyone, you might find another new person who seems nervous, too. You can sympathise with them because you share the same feeling.

Or suppose your friend is feeling sad because their bunny has died. You might be sad about it, because your friend is sad, and maybe you miss the bunny, too.

Sympathy is very nice because you understand what the other person is feeling as you feel it too.

Empathy

Now let's do something very clever: let's clear up the difference between *empathy* and *sympathy*.

Sympathy

Empathy is when you care about what someone else is feeling, even though you don't feel the same thing. You empathise with them because you can imagine what's going on for them and how they feel. *Sympathy* is when you share the same feelings as someone else.

Got it? Kind of? You deserve a medal. It can be quite tricky to understand the difference between empathy and sympathy and it's ok to mix them up sometimes. Both are important tools in understanding how someone else feels.

Showing empathy

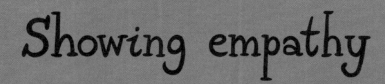

Maybe sometimes you feel bothered and cross and you just want to shout at the whole world. Someone might say, 'Stop being so grumpy!' and that doesn't help at all. What does help (a bit) is when someone else says, 'You poor thing, I feel like that sometimes, too.'

Feeling understood helps to show you that your feelings are normal and OK, and that you aren't alone. And actually, that might help you calm down a bit.

That's empathy. When someone shows empathy, they show that they understand how you're feeling and they don't think you're silly. It can be a big relief to feel that someone understands and that you aren't alone with your feelings. And that can help to make you feel a little better.

Why is empathy important?

Empathy is one of the most important things in the whole world. It connects people and makes us all feel understood and valued. Sometimes people keep their feelings hidden because they worry that no one will understand how they feel. It can make them feel lonely or hurt. But showing empathy helps people to feel that they are not alone, that their feelings are important, perfectly normal and understood.

We want to live in a world where everyone has a lot more empathy for everyone else. That's why we've written this book about how to understand other people's feelings.

Do you need to feel the same way?

It's possible to empathise with someone even if you've never felt the same way as them. But it's easier if you have shared the same experience.

Have you ever bumped your 'funny bone' on your elbow and it really hurt? It's actually a nerve rather than a bone, but it's sensitive and can be really painful if it gets knocked. If you've experienced this, you'll find it easier to *empathise* when it happens to a friend. You'd say, 'I know, it hurts so much doesn't it. I know what you're feeling, I've felt that too – it's horrible.' You *connect* with what they're feeling because you've felt it too. You can easily remember how painful it is.

However, maybe you've never hit your funny bone, so you don't actually know how unpleasant and unusual it is. But that doesn't mean you can't empathise. You can still imagine that it's very painful and, even if you don't know that particular pain, you know that the person is suffering. You can still make a connection with them in a way that helps them to feel understood.

It's the same with emotions. Suppose you're at school and there's a new child in your class. Perhaps they don't really talk to anyone at first because they feel shy. If you've ever felt shy before, you can empathise with them now. You know how it feels to want to talk to new people but be too worried or self-conscious to say anything. What should you say? What if you say something silly? What if no one wants to be your friend?

You know this child who is feeling shy doesn't need someone to ask them loads of questions all at once or say 'are you always this quiet?' What they need is someone (maybe you) to be gentle and calm, to smile, say 'Hello' and make them feel welcome.

On the blackboard:

$1 \times 11 =$ $6 \times 11 =$

$2 \times 11 =$ $7 \times 11 =$

$3 \times 11 =$ $8 \times 11 =$

$4 \times 11 =$ $9 \times 11 =$

$5 \times 11 =$ $10 \times 11 =$

Who can you feel empathy for?

Sometimes people have experiences – and problems – that aren't much like anything that's ever happened to you.

For instance, you might not know how it feels to have to move to another country. And unless you know someone who has done this, you might not think about it much at all. But if you had to *imagine* what someone in this situation might be feeling, you might think: it must be hard to leave your school and friends behind and to live somewhere completely new.

This is the wonderful thing about empathy: it's not about feeling sorry for someone. Empathy is trying to imagine what it feels like to be someone else.

It is thinking about what is important to them, what they enjoy, what they love and care about and how their experiences might affect them.

Can you imagine being 100 years old? What would that feel like? What would you care about? What would your body be like? It's hard to imagine, but it's interesting, too.

Maybe you would think, 'I used to love running about and jumping over things, but now I can't because my knees get too sore.' Or, 'I used to have soft, smooth skin, but now I have lots of wrinkles.' Or, 'I remember what it was like being eight. I loved drawing and running around with my friends. I never thought I would get old, but now I am.'

You don't really know what it is like to be old yet – but you can probably imagine. And the more you imagine, the more you start to feel empathy. It can help you understand and relate to older people – maybe like your grandparents – and imagine how frustrating it might be to move so much slower than you used to, or how annoying it is to forget things.

Can you feel empathy for someone who isn't very nice?

Sometimes people don't want to empathise with someone because they think it means *agreeing* with how the other person thinks or how they act. They think, 'He's not very kind to other people, so I can't feel empathy for him.' But should we save our empathy for people who are kind and nice? Do other people, who behave in ways that aren't kind, need empathy too?

Understanding how someone feels and why they have ended up feeling that way is not the same as agreeing with them or thinking that it's good that they feel this way. Sometimes people's feelings cause them to behave in ways that are not kind or nice. Having empathy for them can help to understand their behaviour and help them to change it.

You may know this from your own experience. Suppose you have done something not very nice (everyone has). Maybe you were feeling worried or stressed and were mean to your brother, sister or friend when they tried to talk to you. Maybe you shouted at your mum or dad when really all you wanted to do was cry and ask them for a hug because life can be overwhelming sometimes.

When things like that happen, it would be helpful if other people showed empathy for you. If they said, 'I understand that you feel angry. Even though you've done something not very nice, I want to listen to you and help you feel less bad.'

A good person (like you) can sometimes have not very nice feelings. That's totally normal. You don't want another person to say it's OK to act in a not very nice way, but you do want them to understand why you acted like that and listen to you when you say you're sorry.

Other people's feelings aren't always about you!

Suppose you ask your mum if she can help you with something and she says, 'Oh not now!' Or you tell your dad about a problem with your friend and you can see he's not listening. Or suppose you're in a cafe and some people are laughing and one of them looks over in your direction. Or you wave at your friend in the street and they walk right by you and don't smile or say 'Hello'.

When someone else has a feeling, it's normal for us to think that it's *about us*. You might feel:

- Mum seems cross. What have I done wrong?

- Dad doesn't care because I talk too much.

- The people in the cafe are laughing at me.

- My friend is ignoring me because they don't like me anymore.

These are very natural thoughts.
But are they *true*? Almost certainly not.

Maybe your mum just has so many things
to do and feels a bit overwhelmed and
stressed. She's usually keen to help you.

Maybe your dad is distracted because
he has a problem to sort out at work.

Maybe the people at the other table
are laughing at a joke and one of
them looked over at you because
they were worried that they might
be a bit too loud.

Maybe your friend didn't notice
you in the street because they
were daydreaming or thinking about
something that was worrying them.

$$2x + 7y = 5$$

If you had a magic machine for looking inside other people's brains and seeing what they were actually thinking, you'd understand that mostly people's feelings aren't to do with you at all.

The funny thing is you probably know this *from the other side.*

Imagine you are in a restaurant and dad says something really funny and you burst out laughing and then you look round the room because it was a really loud laugh. You'd be so amazed if you found out that someone else was worried you were laughing at them. Of course you weren't. You weren't thinking about them at all.

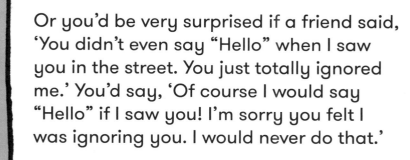

Or you'd be very surprised if a friend said, 'You didn't even say "Hello" when I saw you in the street. You just totally ignored me.' You'd say, 'Of course I would say "Hello" if I saw you! I'm sorry you felt I was ignoring you. I would never do that.'

Now that you understand that other people's feelings aren't always about you, it's good to remember this and try and help other people with their feelings. You could ask Mum if she needs any help with anything or ask Dad 'Are you OK?' You can shout 'Hi' to your friend if they don't see you at first on the street.

And one last thing ...
Feelings can be tricky

You feel all sorts of things. Sometimes nice feelings, sometimes not so nice. And it's like that for other people, too. You are complicated and they are complicated – even if they don't always show it.

But complicated isn't bad. Being complicated makes you interesting. You are lots of things: sometimes cheerful, sometimes weepy, sometimes angry, sometimes kind.

And other people are usually the same. They feel muddled and worried and silly and embarrassed and joyful and fascinated in a great big mix, but you might not guess that straight away from the way they behave. Using your empathy skills to think about how other people might be feeling helps you to be a kinder and more supportive friend to them.

Also available from The School of Life

ISBN: 978-1-915087-27-0

What Are You Feeling?

A picture book of your emotions

An illustrated guide helping children to identify and articulate how they are really feeling.

Feelings can be complicated to understand and difficult to explain. This book helps children to recognise their emotions and to find the words to describe them, in order to understand and manage them.

With beautiful illustrations, this sensitive and engaging book is designed to support the early steps of self-discovery and to create special moments for the sharing of thoughts, feelings, questions and ideas.

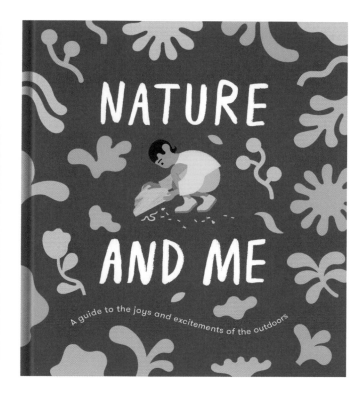

ISBN: 978-1-912891-31-3

Nature and Me

A guide to the joys and excitements of the outdoors

An essential guide to encourage children to explore, enjoy and benefit from the natural world around them.

Children are constantly being told how important nature is and that natural things are good for them. But it's still often hard for them to know why nature might actually be fun, uplifting, consoling – and a real friend for them.

This is a book about how nature can touch us all and help us with our lives (especially when we might be feeling bored, sad or lonely). We learn about the ways in which we can come to love and be inspired by various examples from nature, such as:

- a giant anteater
- a view of the Alps
- a flatfish
- the night sky
- an okapi
- a cuddle with a favourite puppy

In this book, we aren't just lectured to about nature, we are taught to love and connect with it – through beautiful illustrations and a tone that's encouraging, warm and easy for children, and their favourite adults, to relate to.

Also available from The School of Life

ISBN: 978-1-915087-19-5

An Emotional Menagerie

An A to Z of poems about feelings

An imaginative and engaging exploration of childhood emotions through poetry and evocative illustration.

Children experience all sorts of emotions: sometimes going through several very different ones before breakfast. Yet they can struggle to put these feelings into words. An inability to understand and communicate their moods can lead to bad behaviour, deep frustration and a whole host of difficulties further down the line.

An Emotional Menagerie is an emotional glossary for children. A book of 26 rhyming poems, arranged alphabetically, that bring our feelings to life – Anger, Boredom, Curiosity, Dreaminess, Embarrassment, Fear, Guilt, and more.

Filled with wise, therapeutic advice, brought to life through musical language and beautiful illustrations, *An Emotional Menagerie* is an imaginative and universally appealing way of increasing emotional literacy.

ISBN: 978-1-912891-19-1

Happy Healthy Minds

A children's guide to emotional wellbeing

An essential guide to emotional wellbeing for children; tackling everyday issues to facilitate happier, healthier lives.

Our minds are beautifully complicated and brilliant machines. For much of our lives, these machines run efficiently with minimal maintenance. However, just like our other organs, they do require some proper attention every now and then and recognising this at an early age can help as children progress into adulthood.

This is a guide designed to help children become more aware of their emotional needs and examines a range of topics that might give their minds difficulties, for example: when parents don't seem to understand us, when we are finding it hard to make friends, when we feel angry, anxious or lack confidence.

We explore a range of common scenarios encountered by children and talk about some of the very best ideas to help deal with them. By offering a sympathetic and supportive framework, *Happy, Healthy Minds* encourages children to open up, explore their feelings and face the dilemmas of growing up armed with emotional intelligence.

Also available from The School of Life

ISBN: 978-1-9997471-4-5

Big Ideas for Curious Minds

An introduction to philosophy

Accessible philosophy for children; a collection of important concepts from 25 famous thinkers.

Children are, in many ways, born philosophers. Without prompting, they ask some of the largest questions about time, mortality, happiness and the meaning of it all. Yet too often this inborn curiosity is not developed and, with age, the questions fall away.

This is a book designed to harness children's spontaneous philosophical instinct and to develop it through introductions to some of the most vibrant and essential philosophical ideas of history. The book takes us to meet leading figures of philosophy from around the world and from all eras – and shows us how their ideas continue to matter.

ISBN: 978-1-915087-48-5

Big Ideas from Literature

How books can change your world

Introducing children to books through the ages, showing how they can develop both empathy and resilience through exploring the stories they tell.

From an early age, we tend to be told that books matter, but very rarely are we properly allowed to examine why – and therefore we can miss out on a genuine engagement with books. *Big Ideas from Literature* dares to ask the obvious but crucial questions about the whole business of reading: What is reading really for? What are stories trying to do for us? Why should we care?

In a tone that's engaging and playful, we're shown how books help us to grow, why we cry about the fate of certain characters and how to read for genuine pleasure rather than to please a teacher or parent. Along the way, we learn about the history of literature and about some of the many fascinating books from around the world we might enjoy.

Big Ideas from Literature helps us with the greatest challenge we can ever have around books: how to make them into our true friends.

Also available from The School of Life

ISBN: 978-1-912891-20-7

What Can I Do When I Grow Up?

A young person's guide to careers, money – and the future

A unique, illustrated guide to the world of work, bringing clarity to children's essential questions on potential future careers.

Have you ever felt confused, scared or even a little annoyed when an adult has asked, as if it were the most normal thing in the world: What do you want to do when you grow up? If so, you are not alone. Knowing what you want to do with your life is one of the hardest questions you will ever have to answer and it's one that most adults are still grappling with...

What Can I Do When I Grow Up is a book about the world of work written expressly for young people. It takes us on a journey around the most essential questions within the topic, such as: How can I discover my passions? What should a 'good' job involve? How much money should I make? How does the economy work?

The result is a book that will spark exceptionally fruitful conversations and help you look forward to your work life with positivity and anticipation.

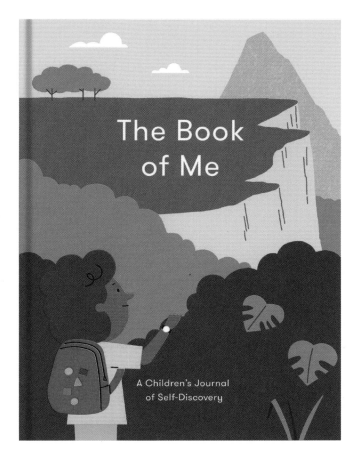

ISBN: 978-1-912891-61-0

The Book of Me

A children's journal of self-discovery

An engaging guided journal for developing children's understanding of themselves and their emotions.

Children love to explore, born with a boundless desire to understand the world around them. While most of the outside world has already been mapped, there's a whole other world that has yet to be discovered, one that's accessible only to them: their own minds.

The Book of Me is a guided journal of self-discovery. It takes readers on a journey inside themselves, helping them explore their mind, their moods, their imagination, their conscience, and how they determine the course of their lives. Alongside wise and engaging explanations of ideas, each chapter contains a wealth of interactive exercises that together help to create a rich and unique self-portrait.

Combining psychology, philosophy and sheer fun, *The Book of Me* is an introduction to the vital art of self-knowledge, showing how it can help us grow into calmer, wiser and more rounded human beings.

To join The School of Life community and find out more,
scan below:

The School of Life publishes a range of books on
essential topics in psychological and emotional
life, including relationships, parenting, friendship,
careers and fulfilment. The aim is always to help
us to understand ourselves better – and thereby to
grow calmer, less confused and more purposeful.
Discover our full range of titles, including books
for children, here:
www.theschooloflife.com/books

The School of Life also offers a comprehensive
therapy service, which complements, and
draws upon, our published works:
www.theschooloflife.com/therapy

www.theschooloflife.com